SportsZone Biographies

KOBE BRYANT

BY LUKE HANLON

SportsZone

An Imprint of Abdo Publishing
abdobooks.com

abdobooks.com

Published by Abdo Publishing, a division of ABDO, PO Box 398166, Minneapolis, Minnesota 55439.

Printed in China.
052023
092023

THIS BOOK CONTAINS RECYCLED MATERIALS

Cover Photo: Wally Skalij/Los Angeles Times/Getty Images
Interior Photos: Jae C. Hong/AP Images, 5; Focus on Sport/Getty Images Sport/Getty Images, 7; Steve Grayson/WireImage/Getty Images, 9; Chris Pizzello/AP Images, 11; Matt A. Brown/Icon Sportswire/Getty Images, 13; Kevin Reece/Icon Sportswire/AP Images, 15; Lucy Nicholson/AFP/Getty Images, 17; Jeff Haynes/AFP/Getty Images, 18; Matt A. Brown/AP Images, 20; Jack Dempsey/AP Images, 23; Filippo Monteforte/AFP/Getty Images, 24; Stan Honda/AFP/Getty Images, 26; Ted Soqui/SIPA USA/AP Images, 29

Editors: Steph Giedd and Charlie Beattie
Series Designer: Karli Kruse

LIBRARY OF CONGRESS CONTROL NUMBER: 2022949109

Publisher's Cataloging-in-Publication Data

Names: Hanlon, Luke, author.
Title: Kobe Bryant / by Luke Hanlon
Description: Minneapolis, Minnesota: Abdo Publishing Company, 2024 | Series: SportsZone biographies | Includes online resources and index.
Identifiers: ISBN 9781098291686 (lib. bdg.) | ISBN 9781098278236 (ebook)
Subjects: LCSH: Bryant, Kobe, 1978-2020--Juvenile literature. | Basketball players --Biography--Juvenile literature. | Basketball guards (Basketball players)--Biography --Juvenile literature. | Professional athletes--Biography--Juvenile literature.
Classification: DDC 796.092--dc23

TABLE OF CONTENTS

Chapter One

HOLLYWOOD ENDING

Some of the biggest stars in the world flocked to the Staples Center in Los Angeles on April 13, 2016. National Basketball Association (NBA) legends, Hollywood celebrities, and famous musicians dotted the stands. The Los Angeles Lakers weren't going to the playoffs. But fans were in Los Angeles to watch the biggest star of the night. Kobe Bryant was playing in his final NBA game. In a city known for entertainment, the shooting guard put on a show.

Heading into the fourth quarter, Bryant had 37 points. But the Lakers trailed the Utah Jazz 75–66. Los Angeles ran its offense through Bryant to get back into the game. With just over three minutes left, the Lakers trailed by 10 despite 45 points from Bryant. He took over the game from there. Bryant's teammates got him the ball on every possession so he could take a shot—and it kept working.

Kobe Bryant salutes the crowd at the Staples Center near the end of his final NBA game on April 13, 2016.

FAST FACT

After Kobe Bryant's final game, he gave a speech to the crowd at the Staples Center. He told the fans how much he loved them for their support over his 20-year career. Bryant ended his speech by saying, "Mamba out," then dropping the mic. Bryant's nickname was "Black Mamba."

Bryant showed off a variety of scoring moves. He drove to the hoop for a reverse layup. When the defense dropped toward the basket, Bryant pulled up for a jump shot. He then hit a three-pointer with just under a minute left to cut Utah's lead to 96–95. Bryant breathed heavily on the bench during a timeout after that possession. The 37-year-old wasn't done yet, though.

After a missed shot by the Jazz, the Lakers put the ball in Bryant's hands again. All 18,997 fans in attendance were on their feet. The arena erupted when Bryant hit a 20-foot jumper to give the Lakers a 97–96 lead. It also gave him 58 points. The next time down the floor, Bryant hit two free throws to finish the game with 60 points and the win. That was by far the most points scored by an NBA player in their final game. And it was a fitting farewell to one of the league's greatest-ever players.

COMING TO AMERICA

Kobe Bean Bryant was born in 1978 in Philadelphia. His father, Joe Bryant, was playing in the NBA at the time. Joe left the United

Kobe's father, Joe Bryant, averaged 8.7 points per game during his eight years in the NBA.

States when Kobe was five and signed with a professional team in Italy. Kobe lived there until he was 13 years old. After returning to the United States, Bryant starred at Lower Merion High School in Ardmore, Pennsylvania, just outside of Philadelphia. He scored 2,883 points in high school, which broke the Philadelphia record set by Basketball Hall of Famer Wilt Chamberlain.

Bryant had enough success in high school that he decided to skip college. Instead, he declared for the 1996 NBA Draft. He was just the sixth player ever to go to the NBA straight from high school. Before Bryant, the move was something only big men had made. Bryant was a 6-foot, 6-inch shooting guard. Many wondered whether he could be successful in the NBA.

FAST FACT

One of Joe Bryant's high school teammates nicknamed him "Jellybean." That nickname stuck throughout his NBA career. It's also the reason Kobe's middle name is Bean.

However, Lakers general manager Jerry West wanted Bryant badly. Unfortunately for West, the Lakers didn't have a high draft pick. So West made a clever trade. He sent his center, Vlade Divac, to the Charlotte Hornets for the 13th pick. The trade took a few weeks to complete, so the Hornets officially drafted Bryant at the June draft. But by mid-July, Bryant was playing for the team he had rooted for all his life.

After being traded to the Los Angeles Lakers in July 1996, Bryant poses with team general manager Jerry West, *left,* and head coach Del Harris, *right*.

The trade also freed up a spot at center for the Lakers. West filled it by signing free agent superstar Shaquille O'Neal. It wouldn't be long before the pair of Bryant and O'Neal was lighting up the NBA world.

Chapter Two

TOP OF THE WORLD

Kobe Bryant had barely turned 18 when he made his NBA debut with the Los Angeles Lakers in 1996. He was the youngest player in league history at the time. But he didn't always play a lot early in his rookie season. Bryant appeared in 71 games in 1996–97 and started in only six. His first start came on January 28, 1997, against the Dallas Mavericks. He finished the game with 12 points in a 102–83 Lakers win. Less than two weeks later, Bryant wowed the crowd at All-Star weekend by winning the Slam Dunk Contest. He soon became a regular for a playoff team.

The Lakers reached the second round, where they faced the powerhouse Utah Jazz. Utah went up 3–1. In Game 5, Bryant struggled to make 4-for-14 from shooting. That included a missed layup at the end of regulation that could have won the game. He also misfired on two game-tying

Kobe Bryant soars toward the basket during his rookie season in 1996–97.

FAST FACT

Bryant's record as the youngest player was broken twice in his lifetime. The second time was by his Los Angeles Lakers teammate Andrew Bynum on November 2, 2005. But even that night Bryant stole the show. He scored 33 points and hit a buzzer-beating overtime game-winner to beat the Denver Nuggets 99–97.

three-point attempts in the final minute of overtime. The Lakers lost 98–93 to end their season.

Even though Bryant had come up short, his teammates praised the young star's fearlessness. In 1997–98 Bryant put that on display again. He started in only one game, but he was an offensive spark plug off the bench. In one game, he scored 25 points in less than 24 minutes. In a December game he topped 30 points for the first time in his career. He did it again three days later. Bryant hopped off the bench and fired away every night. At times, his teammates thought he shot too much. The young player was still learning to work with his team. But Bryant's scoring talent was undeniable.

Fans took notice. Even though he didn't start for the Lakers, Bryant was voted to be a starter at the 1998 All-Star Game. The 19-year-old Bryant became the youngest All-Star in NBA history. And he stood out among the league's best players. His 18 points were the most of anyone in the Western Conference. That year they won 61 games and reached the Western Conference finals. The following year, with Bryant as a starter, Los Angeles bowed out in

Legendary NBA coach Phil Jackson, *right,* helped turn Bryant and the Lakers into champions.

the conference semifinals. But another legendary arrival was about to push Bryant and the Lakers over the top.

The Lakers hired Phil Jackson as head coach before the 1999–2000 season. He had just won six titles with the Chicago Bulls and superstar Michael Jordan. Bryant had been compared to Jordan ever since he entered the NBA. Now Bryant was ready to take his game to the superstar level. He formed a devastating combination with All-Star center Shaquille O'Neal. Bryant averaged more than 20 points per game for the first time. O'Neal led the

FAST FACT

Bryant faced his idol, Michael Jordan, in the 1998 All-Star Game. Bryant led the West with 18 points, but Jordan scored a game-high 23 and led the East to a 135–114 win.

NBA at 29.7 points per contest. The Lakers rolled to 67 wins and a top seed in the Western Conference playoffs.

KOBE TO SHAQ

The relationship between Bryant and O'Neal wasn't always smooth. Both stars wanted to be the team's main man. But they got along well enough to make the Lakers a championship favorite. After winning their first two series, the Lakers faced the Portland Trail Blazers in the conference finals. The series lasted seven games, with Game 7 played in Los Angeles. The Lakers trailed by 15 points early in the fourth quarter. But Bryant and O'Neal led a stirring comeback to give Los Angeles an 83–79 lead with just over a minute left. After a Blazers miss, Bryant brought the ball up the floor. He beat his defender and drove the middle of the lane. As other Portland players collapsed on him, Bryant lobbed the ball up toward the basket. O'Neal leaped and slammed it down. The alley-oop was one of the signature highlights of that season. And it finished off Portland.

Bryant suffered an ankle injury early in Game 2 of the NBA Finals against the Indiana Pacers. It kept him out of Game 3 as well. Indiana won that game to close the series to 2–1. But Bryant returned in a big way in Game 4. His 28 points drove the Lakers to a 120–118 overtime win. Two games later, Bryant put up 26 points and 10 rebounds as the Lakers closed out the series. At 21 years old, Bryant was an NBA champion.

Bryant jumps into the arms of teammate Shaquille O'Neal, *front*, during the final seconds of the Lakers' victory in the 2000 NBA Finals.

THREE-PEAT

After winning in 2000, the Los Angeles Lakers suddenly looked like a potential dynasty. Shaquille O'Neal had been a dominant force for nearly a decade. Now Kobe Bryant had joined him to give Los Angeles a dynamic combination. The team won 56 games in 2000–01 as both stars averaged more than 28 points per game. They still weren't the best of friends, but the relationship worked on the court.

The Lakers didn't lose a game in the first three playoff rounds. Bryant's scoring ability was on full display. He had a playoff career-high 48 points in Game 4 of the second round against the Sacramento Kings. He followed that up with 45 more against the San Antonio Spurs in Game 1 of the Western Conference finals.

In the NBA Finals, Los Angeles faced Bryant's hometown team, the Philadelphia 76ers. Led by star guard Allen Iverson, Philadelphia interrupted the Lakers' perfect run by winning

The Lakers were nearly unbeatable featuring the combination of Kobe Bryant and Shaquille O'Neal during the early 2000s.

the first game in Los Angeles. Bryant fired back in Game 2. He led all scorers with 31 points. After the game, he was asked about going back to Philadelphia. The competitive Bryant said he was returning home "to cut [the 76ers'] hearts out."

The comment angered the famously passionate Philadelphia fans. But Bryant and the Lakers were not fazed. Bryant led Los Angeles with 32 points in Game 3. In Game 4 he came one assist

Bryant makes a move on Philadelphia 76ers defender Aaron McKie during the 2001 NBA Finals.

short of a triple-double. He added 26 points in Game 5. The Lakers won all three, and Bryant celebrated a title in his hometown.

FAST FACT

The 2002 All-Star Game was held in Philadelphia. Kobe Bryant won the game's Most Valuable Player (MVP) Award. But Philadelphia fans remembered his comments from the previous season's Finals and booed him as he was handed the trophy.

The Lakers had a chance at a third consecutive title in 2001–02. But in the Western Conference finals, they faced a stiff test from the Kings.

Bryant and the Lakers were down 3–2 heading into Game 6. Then he and O'Neal turned it on. Los Angeles trailed 94–93 with 1:55 left when Bryant drove the lane and was fouled. He sank two free throws to put Los Angeles ahead for good. He finished with 31 points, 11 rebounds, and five assists in a 106–102 win. Bryant and O'Neal combined for 65 more points in Game 7. The Lakers won 112–106 in overtime.

The Lakers romped in the Finals against the New Jersey Nets. Bryant averaged 26.8 points per game and led Los Angeles in assists. Los Angeles won 4–0.

Bryant and O'Neal had reached the top of the NBA once again. They played so well on the floor together that it seemed they could win championships for years to come. But their relationship off the floor was worse than ever. The two stars had public disagreements even before their first title together.

Bryant would often criticize O'Neal for coming into seasons out of shape. O'Neal still thought Bryant didn't pass enough. Coach Phil Jackson was frustrated with how his two stars behaved. The next year, the bickering Lakers lost in the second round.

Everything reached its boiling point following the 2003–04 season. After an upset loss in the Finals to the Detroit Pistons, it became clear that Lakers owner Jerry Buss would have to choose between Bryant and O'Neal. Buss stuck with the younger Bryant and traded O'Neal to the Miami Heat. Jackson was also fired, though he returned a year later.

Bryant attempts a two-point shot against the Toronto Raptors on January 22, 2006, in which he scored a career-high 81 points in a single game.

8 TO 24

The Lakers missed the playoffs in 2004–05. The next year, Bryant came out firing shots from everywhere. It led to some special performances. On January 22, 2006, Bryant torched the Toronto Raptors for 81 points. After a 26-point first half, he shot 18-for-28 in the second. That included 6-for-11 from three-point range as the Lakers won 122–104. Bryant had recorded the second-highest single-game scoring total in NBA history. He finished the season as NBA scoring champion, averaging 35.4 points per game. But the Lakers lost in the first round of the playoffs. Bryant had become a controversial player. He was a superstar, but he had never won a title without O'Neal. His fans still loved him. Others thought he was still the same selfish shoot-first player he had been a decade earlier.

Bryant did make one big change before the 2006–07 season. His uniform number in the NBA had always been No. 8. He came out that year wearing No. 24. Bryant said the switch was a way for him to evolve and symbolized greater maturity. Bryant won the scoring title again. But the Lakers were bounced in the first round of the playoffs.

FAST FACT

Bryant came up with the nickname "Black Mamba" after watching the 2003 movie *Kill Bill.* The movie is about a group of assassins, one of which is named Black Mamba after a venomous snake. Bryant later said that's the mindset he had while playing basketball.

Chapter Four

MAMBA MENTALITY

The Los Angeles Lakers brought in a new big man to help Kobe Bryant during the 2007–08 season. Pau Gasol came over in a trade with the Memphis Grizzlies. The two paired well together and got along "like brothers," according to Bryant. Gasol was happy to be a playmaker, while Bryant supplied the scoring. Bryant ended the year with his only NBA MVP Award. Los Angeles also rocketed back to the NBA Finals against the Boston Celtics. This was Bryant's big chance. In his first three Finals wins, Shaquille O'Neal had been the series MVP. Now Bryant played as if he was determined to win the award for himself. In doing so, he could prove that he could win it all without O'Neal on the floor. Even better, he could do it against Boston, long the Lakers' fiercest rival. But despite Bryant's 25.7 points per game, the Lakers lost 4–2.

Bryant and Pau Gasol led the Lakers back to the top of the NBA in the late 2000s.

Kobe Bryant puffs out his jersey after the United States defeated Spain in the 2008 Olympic gold-medal game in Beijing, China.

That summer the Olympics were being held in Beijing, China. Four years earlier, a US team without Bryant had won the Olympic bronze medal. This time he signed up, saying, "I'm tired of watching y'all lose." Bryant averaged 15.0 points per game for what was known as "the Redeem Team." The United States reached the gold-medal game, where Bryant was matched up against Gasol and Spain.

Once again Bryant showed his competitive mentality. On the game's first play, Gasol tried to set a screen on Bryant. The American guard blasted right through Gasol, knocking the big man to the floor. It was something Bryant had said he would do to send a message. Here at the Olympics, the two weren't teammates. Team USA won 118–107.

MAMBA'S MOUNTAINTOP

Bryant and Gasol were back to being friends when the NBA season started. The duo led the Lakers to 65 wins. Only two teams in the Lakers' storied history had won more. Bryant's scoring average of 26.8 points was his lowest in six years. But he turned on the offense in the playoffs. Bryant recorded three 40-point games in the first three rounds. Los Angeles battled its way back to the Finals against the Orlando Magic.

Bryant set the tone with 40 points, eight rebounds, and eight assists in Game 1. The Lakers won 100–75. He was Los Angeles's leading scorer in the next four games, too. After the Lakers won the series 4–1, he got his hands on the Finals MVP. Bryant said it was good to have the "monkey off my back."

Earlier in Bryant's career, both Phil Jackson and O'Neal had labeled Bryant as selfish. Now they both congratulated his maturity and success. "He's learned how to be a leader in a way that people want to follow him," said Jackson.

The Lakers reached Finals again the next year. Their opponents were the Celtics. This time the series stretched to seven games. In the final contest, Bryant came out shooting poorly. He finished the game 6-for-24. But up 76–73 with just over one minute left, Bryant helped seal the win with an assist. Pressured by Boston's defense, he found an open Ron Artest, who hit a three-pointer. The Lakers won 83–79, and Bryant had his fifth title.

Bryant was 31 years old in 2010. He led the Lakers back to the playoffs each of the next two seasons. They were on their way again in 2013 when Bryant went

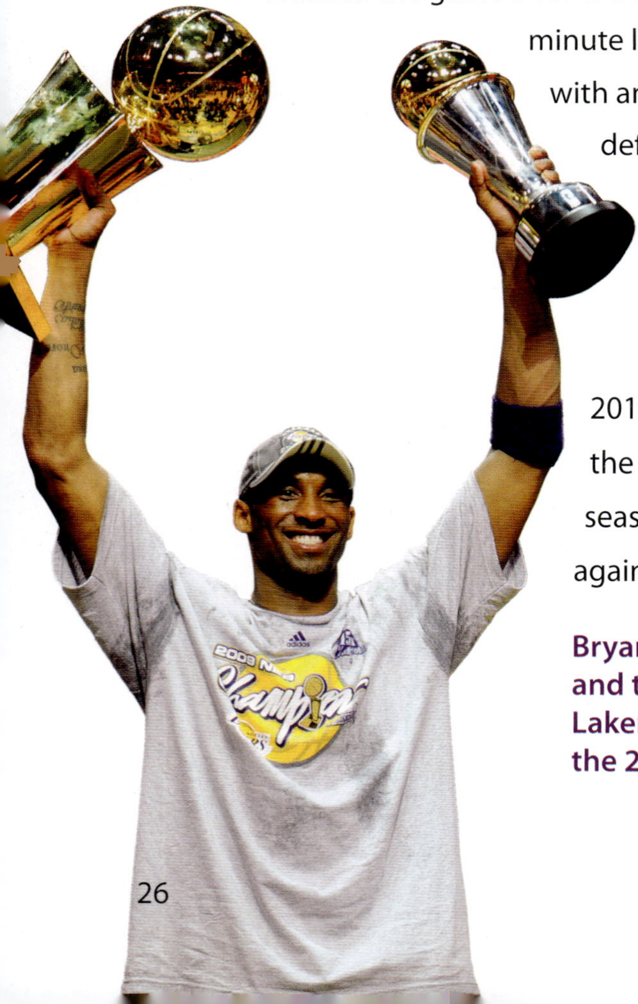

Bryant holds up the NBA Finals trophy and the Finals MVP trophy after the Lakers defeated the Orlando Magic for the 2009 championship.

down with a torn Achilles tendon in an April game against the Golden State Warriors. Even with a devastating injury, Bryant still showcased his competitiveness. He had been fouled on the play and sank two free throws before leaving the game.

Bryant played only 41 games over the next two seasons. He was no longer the superstar he once was, but Bryant became known for his mentorship with young players, often offering them advice and support.

FAST FACT

On November 29, 2015, Kobe Bryant wrote a letter announcing his retirement from the NBA. It was titled "Dear Basketball." In 2017 he adapted that letter into an animated short film. That ended up winning Best Animated Short Film at the 2018 Academy Awards.

Bryant played his final season in 2015–16, ending with his spectacular 60-point game. After he left the NBA, the Lakers retired both of his uniform numbers. He was the first player ever to have two numbers retired by one team. It was a fitting tribute for a player who had led the team to five titles and scored the third-most points in NBA history at the time.

MAMBA FOREVER

Once he stopped playing, Bryant took more time to be with his family. He opened the Mamba Sports Academy in 2018 where he coached his daughter Gianna's youth basketball team. Gianna earned the nickname "Mambacita" because she showcased basketball skills like her father's.

On January 26, 2020, Kobe and Gianna were flying in a helicopter to one of her games when it crashed, killing all nine people on board. The tragedy rocked the sports world. Thousands of fans gathered outside the Staples Center to mourn Bryant. Murals of Kobe and Gianna were painted around Los Angeles. At NBA games over the next few days, teams took intentional 24-second violations on their first possessions. The move was a tribute to one of Bryant's jersey numbers.

A memorial service was held for Kobe and Gianna at the Staples Center on February 24, 2020. Mourners came to honor a player who had been a shining NBA star and one of the greatest winners in the sport's history.

FAST FACT

Michael Jordan and Bryant were publicly viewed as rivals. At Bryant's memorial service, Jordan clarified that the two were great friends. "Everyone wanted to talk about the comparisons between he and I. I just wanted to talk about Kobe," Jordan said.

Shaquille O'Neal speaks to the crowd at Bryant's memorial service on February 24, 2020.

GLOSSARY

alley-oop
When a player catches a pass in the air and scores before landing.

conference
A subset of teams within a sports league.

debut
First appearance.

draft
A system that allows teams to acquire new players coming into a league.

dynamic
Energetic and exciting; in sports, usually referring to an athlete with one or more outstanding skills.

playoffs
A set of games played after the regular season that decides which team is the champion.

rival
An opponent with whom a player or team has a fierce and ongoing competition.

rookie
A professional athlete in his or her first year of competition.

triple-double
Accumulating 10 or more of three certain statistics in a game.

MORE INFORMATION

BOOKS

Donnelly, Patrick. *Los Angeles Lakers*. Minneapolis, MN: Abdo Publishing, 2023.

Graves, Will. *NBA's Top 10 Duos*. Minneapolis, MN: Abdo Publishing, 2019.

Mahoney, Brian. *GOATs of Basketball.* Minneapolis, MN: Abdo Publishing, 2022.

ONLINE RESOURCES

Booklinks
NONFICTION NETWORK
FREE! ONLINE NONFICTION RESOURCES

To learn more about Kobe Bryant, please visit **abdobooklinks.com** or scan this QR code. These links are routinely monitored and updated to provide the most current information available.

INDEX

ABOUT THE AUTHOR

Luke Hanlon is a sportswriter and editor based in Minneapolis.